501 Hockey Facts for Smart Kids

*The Ultimate
Illustrated Collection
of Surprising Stories and
Fun Ice Hockey Trivia
for Boys and Girls!*

Jamie Lindberg

Your BONUS eBooks

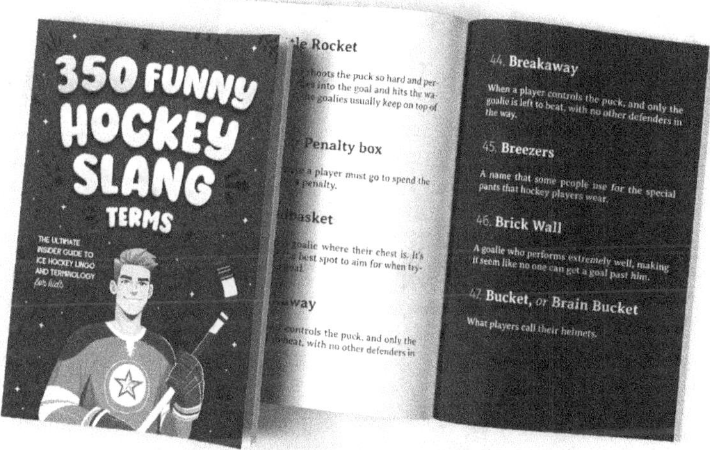

to download them go to

CloudberryPress.com/Hockey

or just scan this qr code
with your phone

Introduction

Welcome to the exciting world of ice hockey! Whether you've been a long-time fan or just recently fallen in love with the sport, you're in for a treat!

Soon, you'll find yourself laughing in disbelief and retelling everyone the most extraordinary stories hockey has to offer!

Did you know that humans are not the only animals that can play ice hockey?

Have you heard about all the surprising adventures players had with the Stanley Cup?

In this book, you'll find 501 fun and interesting bits of trivia, from a variety of world records to the weirdest player superstitions. You'll read about the sport's origin, iconic games, the science and evolution of hockey equipment, and fans so crazy that their names became part of hockey history!

Did you know there was once a coach who was so good at finding game loopholes that the NHL had to change its rules more than once because of him?

You're about to discover all of this and much more!

This book doesn't have to be read in order. Anytime you have a few minutes, just open it on any random page and enjoy the facts.

So, let's dive in!

501 Fun and Interesting Ice Hockey Facts!

1. Games that use sticks and balls have been played for thousands of years all around the world.

2. Polo, a game that has been called "hockey while riding a horse," was already being played in Persia over 2000 years ago!

3. Ice hockey evolved from older games like bandy, hurling, and shinty. These games were played in Britain and Ireland in the 18th and 19th centuries.

4. The British soldiers started playing bandy, the Irish played hurling, the Scots played golf and shinty, and the Dutch played ken jaegen. Some also tried lacrosse. During this period, some of the braver soldiers started playing on skates.

5. Even to this day, the word shinny (based on the Scottish word shinty) is used by Canadians when talking about informal ice or street hockey.

6. The indigenous people of Canada, the Mi'kmaq, also already had their own stick and ball game on ice, called Oochamkunutk!

7. When European soldiers first came to North America, they started playing their home games on frozen rivers and lakes because they were bored and wanted to stay in shape.

8. Ice hockey was invented by all these people from very different cultures mixing their games together.

9. Montreal, in Quebec, Canada, is recognized as the birthplace of our modern version of ice hockey and was very important in its development.

10. No one knows for sure where the word hockey came from. Some think it came from an old French word, "hoquet," a stick shepherds use to care for their sheep.

11. One of the oldest mentions of the word hockey, although in a different form, was in the year 1527, when the people who ruled the city of Galway in Ireland made a rule banning a game called "hokie."

12. James Creighton is considered the "father of ice hockey." He was a Canadian lawyer, journalist, engineer, and athlete.

13. James Creighton organized the first-ever recorded official game of ice hockey! It happened on March 3, 1875.

14. The first game of ice hockey was different from modern hockey. It was played between two 9-player teams (modern hockey is played by 6 vs 6 players), and the goal posts were 8 feet apart (2.4 m) instead of 6 ft (1.8 m).

15. The first hockey club in the world was founded in 1877. It was called the McGill University Hockey Club.

16. Three years later, in 1880, the number of players in each team was changed from 9 to 7.

17. During this period, hockey became so popular and grew so fast that by 1893, there were almost 100 teams just in Montreal!

18. Players from the city of Winnipeg made two important innovations to the game: they started using cricket pads to protect the legs of the goaltender, and they invented the scoop shot, also known as the wrist shot.

19. The people watching the first hockey game were so surprised with how aggressive and violent the game was that some lady spectators even ran away!

20. The ice hockey net was invented by William Fairbrother from Ontario. By 1900, everyone was using them.

21. The "father of ice hockey" in the United States was Malcolm Greene Chace. He was Yale University's first hockey captain.

22. Malcolm Chace also played tennis as an amateur. He was such a good athlete that, at a time, he was ranked as the third-best tennis player in the US!

23. Ice hockey became popular in Europe in the 1920s when it became an Olympic sport. At this time, many bandy players switched to hockey so they could play in the Olympics.

24. The Stannus Street Rink, built in 1897 in Windsor, Nova Scotia, is the oldest surviving hockey rink, but hockey is no longer played there.

25. During these years, all the ice hockey leagues were amateur leagues. People were playing because they loved the game but weren't making money. If the amateur leagues discovered someone was being paid to play, they would actually ban that player!

26. The first professional league was created in 1902. It was called the Western Pennsylvania Hockey League (WPHL).

27. The National Hockey Association (NHA) was formed in Montreal in 1910. In 1917, they changed their name to National Hockey League (NHL) and expanded into the U.S.!

28. Ice skates were invented in Finland over 5000 years ago.
Finns used them during hunts to glide on frozen lakes
and rivers.

29. The first ice skates were not made of metal but of animal
bones. People used the leg bones of horses, oxs, or deer
and tied them to their feet with leather straps. Later,
people started using simple metal blades tied to their
regular shoes with straps or cords.

30. Ice hockey players played with thin pieces of wood as sticks until the 1930s, when they started experimenting with different materials and shapes to improve their performance.

31. In 1948, a Detroit goalie revolutionized the game by inventing the trapper and blocker. He experimented with a rectangular piece of leather and a baseball catcher's glove to create the first specialized gloves for goalies. Before that, all players wore simple leather gloves that offered little protection or control.

32. Jacques Plante was the first goalie to wear a mask during all his games. He decided to do this after he got hit in the face by the puck and got injured. Some people thought Plante was not brave or committed enough, to which he replied that playing without a mask was like jumping from a plane without a parachute: stupid, not brave.

33. Today, fiberglass masks are no longer used, but they have stayed famous because of their use in popular culture. The best-known example is the Friday the 13th horror movies!

34. In 1989, Clint Malarchuk suffered such a dangerous injury to his neck that goaltender masks changed and started including a plastic extension to protect the neck.

35. Before masks were invented, goaltenders used to stand up most of the time because they feared getting hit in the head by the puck. The invention of masks changed the way goalies play. Now, they make much more saves while being on their knees.

36. Goaltender Gerry Cheevers had a unique way of decorating his mask. Every time his mask was hit by a puck or a stick, he would draw a stitch mark on it to show where he would have been injured without the mask.

37. Another strategy that became possible with the invention of masks was to use the head to stop shots. This is a rare move, but it has been used successfully by goalies like Henrik Lundqvist and Dominik Hašek!

38. Kenneth William Clay invented the hockey visor after becoming blind in his left eye after being hit with a stick. The invention was very controversial at the time, with people calling it a "wrap-around windshield" and "fish bowl."

39. One of the first players to wear a helmet was Jack Crawford. He did it to hide his bald head!

40. In 1979, John Ziegler, president of the NHL at the time, made it mandatory for all new players to start wearing helmets. The rule allowed older players to continue not wearing helmets if they didn't want to.

41. A sweater is another name for the jersey that ice hockey players wear. This comes from the old days of the sport when people played outside in the cold winter and needed wool-knit sweaters to keep them warm.

42. In ice hockey, players wear jerseys with numbers to identify themselves. However, the National Hockey League does not allow some numbers. The NHL has banned using 0 and 00 for jerseys because they cause problems with the league's database system!

43. Until 1964, almost all goalies would have a jersey with the number 1. The tradition started changing when teams began to require two goaltenders since they couldn't both have number 1.

44. In the past, goalie pads were made of leather and horsehair, which would soak up water from the ice and freeze. This made the pads very heavy and hard to move in. Nowadays, goalie pads are made of lightweight synthetic

materials that repel water, making them easier to wear and more flexible.

45. During the 1990s, hockey jerseys became popular in hip-hop culture when Snoop Dogg wore one in the music video for his "Gin and Juice" song!

46. In most professional Ice Hockey leagues, players must wear a unique device called a "fight strap." It attaches the jersey to the inside of the pants and prevents an opponent from pulling the jersey over the player's head during a fight. Before "fight straps" were invented, it was common for fights to end with the jerseys wrapped around the players' heads and everyone fighting blind!

47. The word jockstrap comes from "jockey strap." Jockstraps were originally made to increase comfort for people who rode bikes for work, like messengers and deliverymen - "bike jockeys."

48. In the past, many hockey players didn't have front teeth because of hits and fights. Now, most players wear mouthguards that protect their teeth and jaw.

49. When the mouthguard was first invented, it was called a "gum shield"!

50. Hockey skates are different from figure skates in two ways. First, they have a rounded heel for better maneuverability and agility. Second, they don't have toe picks, which are small spikes on the front of the blade, because toe picks can cause injuries if players crash into each other on the ice.

51. Ice hockey skates need to be sharpened often to help players skate faster and smoother. A professional player will
sharpen their skates hundreds of times in their career.

52. Shin guards have a very ancient origin. The first mention
of shin guards in history is in the Bible, where it says that
the famous Goliath, a giant warrior, wore leggings made
of bronze. That means shin guards have been around for
thousands of years!

53. The machine that smooths the ice on a hockey rink is called an ice resurfacer. It was invented by a man named Frank Zamboni in 1949 in California. He was the first to make a machine that could clean and freeze the ice in one pass. That's why some people call it a "Zamboni" after him.

54. Before the invention of the ice resurfacer, it took a lot of work and time to resurface a rink. Three or four workers had to scrape off the old ice and wash it. Then, they had to spray a thin layer of water to create fresh ice.

55. Puck is a word that comes from Scottish Gaelic and Irish languages. It means to hit or push something hard with a stick. It comes from the same root as the verb "to poke."

56. Pucks are made of rubber and frozen before the game to reduce bouncing during play.

57. The first pucks ever used were made from frozen cow dung! These pucks were not very durable – they could only be used for one game before they lost their shape and hardness – so people quickly switched to wooden pucks.

58. The first pucks were not round but square! It was only in 1880 that the first round pucks were invented.

59. The original puck used in the first organized ice hockey game was made from cutting down a lacrosse ball. It was made from soft rubber, which made it much bouncier than a modern puck.

60. Some players use pucks made of steel to increase their wrist strength. These pucks can't be used for shooting because they're too dangerous.

61. When a player hits the puck, it can reach up to 100 miles per hour (160 km/h) or even faster. Denis Kulyash of Avangard Omsk, Russia, hit the fastest ice hockey shot recorded in a competition. His slapshot achieved a speed of 110.3 mph (177.5 km/h)!

62. Ice Hockey players use sticks that are specially made for them. The sticks can have different sizes and shapes,

depending on the player's height, weight, and personal preference. No standard size or shape exists, so each player can choose what works best for them.

63. The first hockey sticks were created by a famous and influential Mi'kmaqs named Joe Cope, known for his talent at carving wood!

64. The oldest known hockey stick was made in the 1830s. It was made from sugar maple wood, a type of tree that grows in Canada. The stick is now displayed at the Canadian Museum of History.

65. The most expensive ice hockey stick in history was sold in 2006 for $2.2 million. It was made in the 1850s, and, at the time, it was thought to be the oldest in the world. It's now estimated to be worth over US$4 million.

66. In the early days of ice hockey, players used heavy, stiff wooden sticks that lasted a long time. One famous player, Moose Johnson, had a stick that was so long that he could reach almost 100 inches (2.5 meters) on the ice. He never changed his stick in his whole career.

67. The angle between the shaft and the blade of a hockey stick is called the lie. Different players use different lies depending on their height and skating posture.

68. Today's hockey stick blades are curved, but they were not always like that. In the late 1950s, a player named Andy Bathgate started to "break" his stick blades on purpose to make them curvy. He discovered that this made his slap shots fly in unpredictable ways, which could confuse the goalies and defenders.

69. Bobby Hull, a famous NHL player, popularized curved blades in the 1960s. He called them "banana blades". Since these curved blades made the slap shots fly faster and more unpredictably, they became very dangerous for the goalies who did not wear masks back then.

70. Because of this, the NHL created a rule that the blades of the hockey sticks cannot be too curved. A player who uses a stick with too much curvature gets a two-minute penalty!

71. Some people think the curvature rule shouldn't exist because, nowadays, the curve does not make a big difference in the game. Some coaches have also used this rule to get an advantage over their opponents by asking for a stick check during essential moments.

72. A hockey rink's surface is white because it's painted! Otherwise, it would be transparent. This makes it easier for players and watchers to see the puck and lines.

73. The first Zamboni was not like the ones we see today. It was made using parts from an old army vehicle and could turn all four wheels simultaneously. This made it easier to move around the ice, but it also made it harder to stop. So, sometimes, the Zamboni would get stuck against the walls of the ice rink! Because of this, Frank Zamboni changed the machine so that only the front wheels could turn.

74. During the 1992 Winter Olympics, French figure skater Laëtitia Hubert fell so often that she was nicknamed "Human Zamboni"! Since then, the word Zamboni has been used to tease or mock someone constantly falling on the ice.

75. The red light behind the NHL nets was created by Arthur Sicard. He came up with the idea in 1938 to help the fans see when a goal was scored without waiting for the referee to confirm it.

76. The "glass" around hockey rinks is not really glass. It's a special plastic called Plexiglas that can resist high impacts, such as pucks flying at high speeds or players crashing into it. This way, the fans can watch the game safely and clearly.

77. Bobby Hull was a famous left winger. He once hit a slapshot so hard that he broke a wooden rink barrier! This event helped make the NHL start using Plexiglas instead.

78. The walls around a hockey rink do more than keep the puck in. They're made to be springy to soak up the force when players bump into them. This helps keep the players from getting hurt.

79. The Stanley Cup is the oldest trophy still given to North American sports teams!

80. In 1889, Lord Stanley of Preston, the Governor of Canada at the time, went to a Winter Carnival and saw a game of ice hockey for the first time there. He and his family liked the game so much that his sons convinced him to donate a trophy to the hockey championship.

81. In 1893, the "Dominion Hockey Challenge Cup" was awarded to the Montreal Hockey Club for the first time. The trophy later became known as the Stanley Cup!

82. Lord Stanley's son and daughter were also important figures in hockey. His son Arthur helped to create the Ontario Hockey Association. His daughter Isobel was one of the first women to play ice hockey!

83. When the Stanley Cup was first awarded over 100 years ago, it was made entirely of silver and was only 7 inches tall (18 cm)!

84. Lord Stanley bought the original cup for ten guineas, the name of the coins used then. When converted and adjusted to our current time, it equals $1,585 US dollars!

85. Many people call the cup a punch bowl, but it was actually a rose bowl, according to silver expert John Culme.

86. The current Stanley Cup is made from silver and nickel, is almost 3 feet tall (90 cm), and weighs nearly 35 lbs (15 kg)! On top, the actual cup part of the trophy is a copy of the original bowl.

87. The Stanley Cup has traveled to many military bases around the world. The cup has been used to boost the soldiers' morale and show appreciation for their service. No trophy in the world has traveled as much as the Stanley Cup.

88. The Stanley Cup is unique among the major sports trophies in North America because, unlike other sports trophies, a new one is not made every year. Instead, the same cup is passed on from one winner to another. The teams that win the cup get to keep it for a while during the summer and some days in the season, but they have to return it eventually.

89. Another thing that makes the Stanley Cup different from other trophies is that every year, the names of some of the winning players, coaches, management, and staff are engraved on the cup.

90. Since the cup didn't have enough room for everyone's names, it was changed to have 5 "bands." Each band has space for the names of 13 winning teams. After 13 years, when the most recent band is complete, the top band is removed, put for display at the Hockey Hall of Fame in Toronto, and a new empty band is added to the bottom.

91. More than three thousand different names have been engraved in the Stanley Cup!

92. The Stanley Cup has many nicknames, such as The Cup, The Holy Grail, or even Lord Stanley's Mug, as a joke.

93. The Stanley Cup wasn't awarded in 1919 because of the Spanish Flu epidemic.

94. The Montreal Canadiens have won the Stanley Cup 24 times – more than any other team in history!

95. There are fifteen women whose names appear on the Cup. The first woman to achieve this honor was Marguerite Norris, the President of the Detroit Red Wings when they won the Cup in 1954 and 1955.

96. Before people started removing the top band, the Stanley Cup grew bigger every year because a new band was added for each winner. At a certain point, it got so big that people started calling it "Stovepipe Cup," saying it looked like a stove's exhaust pipe!

97. There have been many engraving mistakes over the decades. Dickie Moore won the Cup six times in his career. Each time, his name was spelled differently on the trophy!

98. The Winnipeg Victorias started one of the oldest traditions in ice hockey in 1896. They were the first team to celebrate their victory by drinking champagne from the top bowl of the trophy! This custom has been followed by many champions ever since.

99. A new tradition was born in 1950 when Ted Lindsay, a player from the Detroit Red Wings, lifted the Stanley Cup and skated around the rink. He was the first one to do that after winning the championship. Now, every winning team captain follows his example and celebrates with the trophy above his head.

100. Many NHL players believe that touching the Cup before winning it will bring bad luck, so they avoid it at all costs.

101. After winning the Stanley Cup, many players have unofficially spent a private day with the cup. This tradition began in 1995 with the New Jersey Devils.

102. Some players have done very unusual things with the cup, like Ken Daneyko, who once used it as a bowl for his cereal!

103. Derian Hatcher filled it with ice and drinks and used it as a cooler at a party!

104. Clark Gillies once let his dog eat from the Stanley Cup!

105. Dustin Brown, the captain of the Los Angeles Kings, celebrated his victory by letting his two older sons drink chocolate milk from the cup!

106. The Colorado Avalanche is the only team in the NHL that has never lost when they have reached the Stanley Cup Finals. Every time they have played in the Finals, they have won the championship!

107. In April 2006, 114 years after its creation, the Stanley Cup returned to London, where it was originally made, and a commemorative plaque was installed at the store site where Lord Stanley bought the iconic trophy.

108. Tomas Holmström, a former Swedish player who won the Cup four times with the Detroit Red Wings, let his cousin Robert baptize his daughter with the Cup!

109. Game 3 of the 1975 Stanley Cup Finals is famous as "The Fog Game" because a heavy fog covered the ice, making it difficult for players to see. In addition to the fog, a bat was flying around inside the arena during the game!

110. The ice quality in an ice hockey rink can drastically change the game. Players even came up with their own terms for it, calling it "fast ice" if it's smooth and quick and "slow ice" if it's rough and makes the puck move slower.

111. Back in the day, people thought the slickness of ice came from pressure or friction melting the ice to form a slippery layer. But recently, scientists have figured out skates and pucks just don't press down hard enough to make ice melt on the spot. Instead, they found that ice naturally has a "quasi-fluid layer" on its surface. This layer is not exactly ice or liquid water, and it's super slippery. Ice has this layer even when extremely cold, like -200 °F (-129 °C).

112. Ice can change its quality during the game, affecting how it is played. Teams even adapt their strategy depending on how good the ice is. They often go for safer plays instead of fancier moves when dealing with "slow ice" or "bad ice."

113. To keep the ice speedy for hockey, it's usually chilled to 16 °F (-9 °C) but bumped to 22 °F (-5.5 °C) for figure skaters, who like their ice a bit softer for smoother landings.

114. Hockey rinks make ice by freezing saltwater that flows through pipes in a big concrete base called the "ice slab." Once this base gets really cold, they add several thin layers of water on top. After a few layers, they paint all the game lines and ads onto the surface. Then, they seal it up with 8 to 10 more layers of ice. The final ice thickness is just around one inch (2.5 cm)!

115. Skating is the fastest method to move across the earth's surface while on your feet! Unlike running, where each step slows you down, skating has almost no friction, so one foot pushes while the other glides smoothly.

116. Skate blades in ice hockey are made with a concave surface, not flat. A process called hollow-grinding carves out the center steel and creates two sharp edges that allow

players to grip the ice better when they need to stop, start, or make quick turns.

117. NHL hockey players can skate incredibly fast, moving over the ice at over 20 miles per hour (32 km/h). The fastest skaters can even hit speeds above 30 miles per hour (48 km/h)!

118. Hockey goalies have to block pucks flying at speeds over 100 mph (160 km/h), wearing 50 pounds of gear (22 kg). Their natural genetic ability and rigorous training allow them to react to a shot in as little as 150 milliseconds.

119. Goalies often have superstitions. Patrick Roy, one of the greatest goalies, used to talk to his goalposts during games because he thought they could help him block the puck!

120. Flow (also called "being in the zone") is a state in psychology in which a person is fully immersed and focused on an activity, enjoying it and performing it with high skill and without feeling the passage of time. Many hockey players experience feeling "in the zone," which is one reason they love playing hockey.

121. When a goalie is in "flow," they can feel like the game is moving slower, and the hockey puck looks bigger, making it easier to stop. Some goalies feel like their hand moves by themselves to catch the puck. They might even be surprised by their own great saves!

122. Hockey uses special design tricks from engineering to make the stick flex just the right way. When players take a shot, the stick flex stores up energy. When the stick snaps back, that energy is released, sending the puck flying incredibly fast across the ice. When this is done right, the puck moves faster than almost any object in major team sports!

123. Hockey gear often has special coatings to keep bacteria from growing! This shows how important chemistry is for keeping sports equipment clean and keeping athletes healthy.

124. The shape of a hockey stick blade changes how a puck moves by making the puck spin in the air. When the puck spins fast, it can curve while flying because of the Magnus effect. This makes it harder for goalies to guess where it will go and to stop it.

125. After playing a hard game, most players use a stationary bicycle for thirty minutes. This light exercise helps them get rid of the lactic acid that was created inside their muscles.

Lactic acid is what makes muscles feel sore. Riding the bike moves the blood around and cleans the lactic acid out of the muscles.

126. Synthetic ice is a type of plastic engineered to be almost as slippery as natural ice. This makes it possible to practice ice hockey in places where it wouldn't be possible to keep an ice surface frozen.

127. In a typical game, some players lose between 5 and 8 pounds (2 to 3 kg). Most of this is water. That's why it's vital for players to drink enough water and stay hydrated.

128. Linda Sinrod is the oldest female hockey player in the world. She started playing ice hockey at age 35 and continues playing at 82!

129. Jim Harrison and Darryl Sittler share the record for the most points scored by a person in a professional ice hockey game, with ten points each!

130. Gordie Howe from Canada holds the record for the most professional ice hockey games played. In his entire career, he has played 2421 games!

131. The first ice hockey video game sold to the public was called "Ice Hockey." It came out for the Atari 2600 in 1981, made by Activision. The game lets one person play alone, or two people play against each other. Each team had two players – one for attacking and one for defending.

132. Brian Gionta from the USA is the shortest active player in the NHL. He is 5 feet 7 inches tall (170 cm)!

133. Every year, many hockey teams have an event called the "Teddy Bear Toss." Fans throw teddy bears onto the ice when the home team scores their first goal. People collect these toys and give them to charities for children.

134. Mike Sillinger from Canada set a record in the National Hockey League as the player who played for most teams. He played for 12 different teams over his 17-year career!

135. Jessup Hutcheson set the record for the most pucks balanced on the blade of a stick. He was able to balance 25 pucks!

136. The Stanley Cup once enjoyed Los Angeles' celebrity glamour when it was taken on a roller coaster ride at Universal Studios Hollywood!

137. In 1961, during the final playoff game, the Montreal Canadiens were losing against the Chicago Blackhawks. A fan of the Montreal team, not happy with what he was seeing, left his seat and went to the area where the trophy was displayed. He broke the case holding the Stanley Cup and tried to steal it! He got caught, and the police arrested him. When he went to court, he told the judge, "Your Honor, I was simply bringing the Cup back to Montreal where it belongs."

138. The biggest hockey stick in the world is 205 feet (62 m) long and weighs 62,000 pounds (28 tonnes). Canada's government ordered it for the Canadian Pavilion at the 1986 Expo in Vancouver, Canada.

139. The top Finnish hockey league, Liiga, has a unique "Joker" card rule. Teams can use this to let young players join for some games! This helps new stars get better faster.

140. Hockey players often get "skatebite." This pain happens when they tie their skates too tight, and their feet's nerves and blood vessels get squeezed. This shows why it is essential to have sports gear that fits well.

141. Women started playing ice hockey in the late 1800s. The first known game for women happened in 1892 in Barrie, Ontario. In this game, the women wore costumes with long skirts and used a wooden puck.

142. The Preston Rivulettes started in 1931. They were such a successful women's hockey team that they won 96% of their games!

143. The National Women's Hockey League (NWHL) started in the United States in 2015. It was the first women's professional ice hockey league to pay its players. However, these players earn much less than male hockey players.

144. Women who play ice hockey usually have to work full-time jobs because they don't earn enough money from the sport.

145. Art Ross was the first official coach of an NHL team. He coached the Boston Bruins in 1924. Before that, team captains often acted as coaches.

146. NHL coaches often watch and analyze lots of video clips from previous games. They do this to look closely at plays and improve their strategies.

147. In 1982, in Vancouver, coach Roger Neilson started the famous "Towel Power" by waving a white towel on a hockey stick to pretend to give up. He did this to complain about the referees. Now, fans regularly use this symbol to support the team.

148. Scotty Bowman has the most wins of any coach in the NHL regular season, with 1,244 victories! He is famous for winning the Stanley Cup nine times as a coach. He did it with three different teams.

149. Emile Francis changed coaching by using "morning skates" on game days, where players skate for about 20 to 30 minutes in the morning before an evening game. The purpose of morning skates is to activate the muscles, warm up the body, and prepare mentally for the game. Now, this is a common practice in the NHL.

150. Fred Shero coached the Philadelphia Flyers when they were called the "Broad Street Bullies." He liked to use psychology in his coaching. He would sometimes leave philosophical notes with deep thoughts for his players in the locker room.

151. Al Arbour coached the New York Islanders for many years. He helped them win the Stanley Cup four times in a row in the early 1980s. People knew him as a calm and strategic coach. When he was 75 years old, in 2007, he came out of retirement to coach one last game. This made him the oldest head coach in ice hockey history!

152. In 2016, P.K. Subban, a defenseman for the Montreal Canadiens, promised to raise $10 million for the Montreal Children's Hospital. This was the biggest charitable donation by a Canadian athlete!

153. Since 1998, the "Hockey Fights Cancer" campaign, run by the NHL and NHLPA, has collected more than $28 million. This money helps cancer research centers, children's hospitals, and charities supported by players.

154. Wayne Gretzky, known for being very sportsmanlike, deliberately did not score into an empty net once. He did this because he was close to breaking the record of a player about to retire, and he wanted that player to keep the honor!

155. NHL star Sidney Crosby often visits young hockey fans and gives them surprise gifts! He invites them to games and gives them signed equipment.

156. The "Learn to Play" program, backed by the NHL and NHLPA, gives young children free equipment and hockey lessons. It makes start playing the sport more accessible for kids from all backgrounds.

157. Tony Esposito made the butterfly style famous for goalies in the 1960s. In this style, goalies drop to their knees and spread their legs to make a shape like a butterfly. They do this to stop low shots. Now, goalies commonly use this technique.

158. Dominik Hasek was called "The Dominator." He used such a different style to stop the puck that it almost looked like he was doing acrobatic tricks! This unique way of playing helped him win many MVP awards.

159. Goalies say success comes from staying calm and predicting the play. Martin Brodeur, who has the most NHL wins, believes in this. He says it's a mind game for goalkeepers.

160. The shortest player to ever play in the NHL was goalkeeper Roy "Shrimp" Worters, who was only 5'3" (160 cm). He was famous for his agility. He was also the first goalkeeper to get the Hart Trophy MVP award.

161. Billy Smith was the first goalie in the NHL to score a goal and have it on his record. However, it was an own goal! The other team shot the puck, but he was the last to touch it.

162. A funny moment happened in coaching history when Roger Neilson, the coach for the Philadelphia Flyers, got kicked out of a game and returned to the bench wearing a disguise!

163. Ron Hextall was the first NHL goalie to score a goal against an opposing team. He did it by shooting the puck

into the other team's empty net. This proved that goalies can score goals as well!

164. The Finnish winger Jarkko Ruutu, famous for his trash-talking, once bit another player!

165. Bobby Orr is known as an incredible hockey player. He changed how defense is played by scoring 139 points in the 1970-71 season. No other defenseman has scored that many points in one NHL season!

166. Zdeno Chara is the tallest player that has ever played in the NHL, at 6'9" (205 cm)! This height made it very hard for other players to move the puck past him because of his long reach on defense.

167. Bill Gadsby was a courageous defenseman in hockey. He played at a time when the game was very tough. During his career, he got over 600 stitches in his face!

168. On December 11, 1977, Tom Bladon of the Philadelphia Flyers amazed everyone in hockey. He set a lasting record for defensemen by scoring 4 goals and making 4 assists, getting 8 points in one game.

169. Wayne Gretzky scored 2,857 points in his career, and most people think he is the best center the NHL has ever seen. Because of this, they call him "The Great One."

170. In 2009, Sidney Crosby was only 21 when he became the youngest captain to win the Stanley Cup! He showed outstanding leadership and skill playing as a center for the Pittsburgh Penguins.

171. Maurice "Rocket" Richard was a famous right winger. He was such a fan favorite that when he got suspended in 1955, it caused a riot in Montreal!

172. Gordie Howe built bombers during the Second World War. Even though Howe was signed by the Red Wings, he was still a teenager and had to work in a factory during the war. He helped build B-29 bombers at the Ford plant in Dearborn, Michigan. He worked there for two years until he was old enough to play full-time for the Red Wings.

173. In 1979, legendary winger Guy Lafleur was stopped by a police officer for speeding on his way to a game. He told the officer he was late for the game and asked him to escort him to the arena. The officer agreed, and Lafleur made it to the game on time! He scored two goals and one assist in a 6-2 win over the Boston Bruins.

174. Wayne Gretzky, known as the "Great One," always followed the same routine for good luck. He would put on his left skate, then his right skate, then his left pad, and then his right pad. After every period, he would tie his skates again.

175. Sidney Crosby is superstitious about numbers. He wears a jersey number related to his birth date. He also looks for numbers everywhere else in his life – such as when signing contracts and staying in hotels – thinking it might give him an advantage in his career.

176. Maurice "Rocket" Richard was the first player in history to score 50 goals in a single season! He accomplished this in only 45 games, as he missed five games due to injuries, including a broken ankle. However, the NHL counts his record as 50 goals in 50 games since he scored his last goal in the season's final game. Richard's performance set a new standard for excellence in hockey.

177. Gordie Howe almost killed a Member of the Royal Canadian Mounted Police once! When he was 14, Howe played in a senior league game in Saskatoon that turned into a brawl involving fans and police. Howe hit an RCMP officer in the head with his stick, knocking him out. When he saw the yellow stripe on the officer's pants, he realized the man was a cop and escaped the arena before he was arrested!

178. The famous winger Jaromír Jágr had his own brand of peanut butter in the 1990s called Jágr Creamy Peanut Butter! He used to joke that rubbing the peanut butter on his body helped him heal from his injuries.

179. Players often feel very attached to their jersey numbers. They can feel so strongly about a number that they are willing to pay a lot of money or do favors to get it.

180. In 2011, the Tampa Bay Lightning put two machines called Tesla coils inside their arena. These machines would shoot lightning bolts every time the team scored a goal!

181. Ryan Jeffries, a fan, once walked for over 550 miles (885 km) to watch an Oilers game against the Colorado Avalanche! He undertook this to gather funds and awareness

for mental health and suicide prevention. His inspiration was the Oilers' captain, Connor McDavid, whom he considers his hero. Before the game, Jeffries met McDavid and other players, received a signed jersey, and watched the game from a suite with family and friends.

182. John Boutet, a loyal Buffalo Sabres fan, has attended every home game since March 31, 1996, a streak of over 900 consecutive games! He is also a collector of Sabres memorabilia and has a room full of jerseys, pucks, sticks, and other items. He is known as the "Super Fan".

183. The NHL introduced a rule in 1956 that allowed a goal to count even if the net was dislodged, as long as the puck would have entered the net under normal circumstances. The Montreal Canadiens GM proposed the rule after a riot in 1955 that was partly triggered by a disallowed goal by the Canadiens. The rule aimed to prevent teams from knocking off the net on purpose and to reduce the number of disputes over such situations.

184. Wayne Gretzky, the greatest ice hockey player of all time, was so dominant in 4-on-4 situations that the NHL changed the rules in 1985 to make them less frequent! This was known as the "Gretzky rule." He scored over 10% of his total points in 4-on-4 situations in the four seasons before the rule change. The Edmonton Oilers, his team, would intentionally draw coincidental penalties to create 4-on-4 opportunities.

185. In the 2002 Winter Olympics men's ice hockey semifinal between Canada and Belarus, a goal by Belarus was disallowed because the scorer had tucked his jersey into his pants, violating the uniform regulations. This controversial decision, known as the "tuck rule," sparked a debate about the relevance and enforcement of the rule.

186. Maurice Richard once punched a fan who insulted him, resulting in a brawl. But he wasn't sued or arrested because the fan was so proud of the black eye he got from Richard!

187. Hockey player Shaun Van Allen once hit his head so hard during a game that he forgot that he was in the NHL, that he was married, and that he was living his dream of being a professional hockey player! His coach tried to lighten the mood by suggesting they tell Shaun he was the famous player Wayne Gretzky.

188. Famous player Bobby Orr once forgot his socks during a junior game trip and then played so well that he chose to play without socks for the rest of his career!

189. There's a fun tradition in hockey where players stop shaving their beards when the playoffs start, believing it brings good luck, and they only shave after their team is eliminated or wins the Stanley Cup. This "playoff beard" has become a symbol of team unity and superstition in the sport.

190. "Light the lamp" is hockey slang for scoring a goal. It comes from the red light that goes on behind the net when a goal is scored.

191. Ice Hockey player Mark Messier was so popular that he could decide who got into a famous club in New York, even making players from other teams wait outside for hours!

192. The 334 Club is the name given to the 334 fans who attended a New Jersey Devils game on January 22, 1987, despite a severe blizzard. It was the smallest crowd in NHL history. The fans were rewarded with free food, drinks, and tickets. They also received a letter, a T-shirt, and a pin from the Devils. The 334 Club is now a symbol of hockey fan loyalty!

193. A "grenade" is a bad pass that makes it hard for the receiver to control the puck. It usually happens when the passer sends the puck too high or too fast and bounces or rolls on the ice before reaching the intended target.

194. In 1974, the Buffalo Sabres drafted a player that didn't exist! The team's general manager was frustrated with the ridiculously long drafting process, so he decided to have fun and draft a made-up Japanese player called Taro Tsujimoto! Taro Tsujimoto is now a humorous part of the Buffalo Sabres' history and a favorite story among fans.

195. The slang "dirty" is used when a hockey player makes an excellent and skillful move to get past another player.

196. After the Pittsburgh Penguins won the Stanley Cup in 2009, a fan managed to sneak into their celebration

party. Out of everyone at the party, the famous player Mario Lemieux was the only person who noticed that the fan didn't belong there!

197. Winger Dustin Penner once hurt himself while eating pancakes and missed two games because of it!

198. One time, two general managers, Brian Burke of the Ducks and Kevin Lowe of the Oilers, had such a big disagreement over a player contract that Burke went as far as actually renting a barn where they could have a physical fight to settle it! The commissioner of the NHL himself, Gary Bettman, had to step in and stop them.

199. John Garrett, a backup ice hockey goalie for Vancouver in the 1980s, once played a game with a hot dog in his pad! He was used to having someone sneak him hot dogs while he was on the bench, that he would hide inside his pad. One time, during an unexpected call to action, he didn't have time to take the hot dog out and had to play with it inside his pad!

200. An "alley-oop" is slang for when one player throws the puck very high in the air, and another player catches it and scores a goal.

201. Hockey goalie Pelle Lindbergh had a special routine: he wore the same lucky orange T-shirt for every game without ever washing it or fixing it if it got ripped. During breaks, he liked to drink a Swedish beverage with exactly two ice cubes, always taking it with his right hand from the same trainer.

202. The second-quickest hat trick in NHL history was scored
by Jean Béliveau in 1955, taking just 44 seconds during
a power play. His performance was so impressive that it
led to a rule change where now power plays end when
the team with the advantage scores. Béliveau scored a
total of 4 goals in that game. Before this rule change, the
NHL teams voted on it, with the Montreal Canadiens,
Béliveau's team, being the only ones to vote against it.

203. Before a game, as a ritual, Wayne Gretzky often ate four
hot dogs with onions and mustard and drank a Diet Coke.
Sometimes, he chose to have a pizza or sandwich instead,
depending on the location of his team's game.

204. Before games, many hockey players have the superstition of tapping their sticks against something solid a certain number of times because they think this helps them play better on the ice.

205. Brett Hull, a famous ice hockey player, once took his coach's Jaguar car without permission for a night out and ended up breaking the key in the lock. He continued the fun by having an impromptu party with the security staff until a locksmith fixed the car.

206. The "house" is slang for the space in front of the net where most scoring chances happen.

207. One time, during a train journey, Chicago Blackhawks' president Frederic McLaughlin met a man named Godfrey Matheson and was so impressed with his hockey knowledge that he hired him as head coach – even though Matheson had never coached before and didn't know how to skate! Matheson only lasted two games. He lost both.

208. When Clarence Campbell suspended ice hockey player Maurice Richard, people were so upset that they stopped buying Campbell Soup, causing a big dip in sales, even though there was no association between Clarence Campbell and Campbell Soup!

209. A "grocery stick" is slang for a player who is so bad that he never gets to play on the ice. He just sits on the bench and separates the forwards and the defensemen, like a stick that divides the groceries on a conveyor belt at the supermarket.

210. Hockey legend Wayne Gretzky once corrected basketball star Michael Jordan's tipping habits at a poker table in Las Vegas. After Jordan tipped a cocktail waitress a five-dollar chip, Gretzky replaced it with a hundred-dollar chip from Jordan's stack, telling him, "That's how we tip in Las Vegas, Michael."

211. Kevin Bieksa earned his first NHL contract with an unusual story. While trying out for the team, he accidentally got into a fight and knocked out Fedor Fedorov, his teammate, at a local bar. Instead of getting cut from the team, Bieksa was actually signed by the Canucks General Manager, Brian Burke, the very next day!

212. "Chiclets" is a slang term sometimes used jokingly by hockey players to talk about teeth. Because ice hockey is such a physical sport, players sometimes get hit in the mouth and can lose teeth, spitting them out like chiclets.

213. Ivan Hlinka, a famous Czech hockey player and former head coach of the Pittsburgh Penguins, had a habit of taking smoke breaks during the game's intermission, leaving the players to coach themselves. One time, Marc Bergevin, frustrated with the situation, told the arena security that Hlinka was not part of the team and shouldn't be there, leading to the police trying to arrest Hlinka!

214. In ice hockey, an "enforcer" is a player who protects teammates from dirty or violent actions by the other team. They are known for responding strongly, often by fighting or delivering heavy checks, especially if a star player or goalie is targeted. While "enforcer" isn't an official position, these tough players have a special role on their teams, making sure opponents think twice before playing rough.

215. "Breezers" is a name that some people use for the unique pants that hockey players wear.

216. In ice hockey's earlier days, there was a seventh player on the ice called the rover. This player was versatile, helping out on offense and defense whenever necessary.

217. In ice hockey, a "Gordie Howe hat trick" is when a player scores a goal, gets an assist, and has a fight in which they receive a 5-minute penalty in the same game. Although the hat trick is named after the legendary player Gordie Howe, he only accomplished this feat twice during his five-decade-long career and wasn't the first player to do so.

218. Maurice "Rocket" Richard of the Montreal Canadiens once scored a goal despite having a concussion! He was so dazed from a hit that he collapsed on the bench and had to be revived by smelling salts. He went back onto the ice in the game's final minutes and scored the winning goal!

219. Both figure skating and ice hockey were originally part of the Summer Olympics! They made their first appearance in the 1920 Games. However, in 1921, it was decided to create a separate Winter Olympics to include ice and snow sports because they couldn't be easily held in the summer.

220. "Twig" is another name for a hockey stick. The term comes from the fact that hockey sticks used to be made of wood.

221. Jaromir Jagr and Mario Lemieux were legendary hockey players who had a special friendship. They often played practical jokes and once filled a teammate's car with peanuts as a prank!

222. The Swedish word for the mullet hairstyle is "hockey-frilla," which means "hockey haircut"!

223. Wayne Gretzky holds the unique achievement of recording four seasons with over 200 points each – no other player in ice hockey has done this! His average was an astonishing 207 points per season.

224. During the same 5 year span, Wayne Gretzky's team, the Edmonton Oilers, also made history by being the only team to score more than 400 goals for five consecutive years, with a total of 2,114 goals, which is an average of 422.8 goals per season. Gretzky himself scored an average of 75 goals each season during this impressive run!

225. Wayne Gretzky was so incredibly skilled that when he retired, the NHL decided that no other player would ever wear his jersey number, 99, ever again. As a result, the league retired his number for all teams, making him the only player in NHL history to receive this honor.

226. A "play-maker" is slang for someone who can control the puck well and set up their teammates for scoring chances. They are good at skating, stickhandling, and passing but don't shoot often or score many goals.

227. Ice hockey legend Wayne Gretzky is not just the fastest player to reach 1,000 career points; he also holds the record for being the second fastest! He achieved his second set of 1,000 points (from 1,001 to 2,000) faster than any other player has reached their first 1,000 points. No other player in the sport's history has ever reached 2,000 points.

228. Romania played in their first ice hockey World Championship in 1931 and lost 0-15 against the US. After the game, their captain thanked the referee and asked him to write on the official game sheet: "Thank you for playing against us. We have learned a great deal from this game."

229. Wayne Gretzky is the author of the famous inspirational quote, "You miss 100% of the shots you don't take."

230. A "beautician" is slang for a player who is skilled at playing hockey and is also considered attractive and charming!

231. Nathan MacKinnon and Cale Makar from the Colorado Avalanche became a surprising pair. Although they had different ages, they regularly played intense ping-pong matches before games! They thought these matches would bring them good luck.

232. Someone once threw a real octopus on the ice at a Detroit
     Red Wings playoff game! This started a tradition in 1952.
     The octopus has eight legs, representing the eight wins
     needed to get the Stanley Cup back then.

233. Frank McGee, an ice hockey player who was blind in one
     eye, set a record for the most goals in a Stanley Cup game
     by scoring 14 goals against the Dawson City Nuggets!

234. The USSR thought they would win the 1957 Ice Hockey World Championships in Moscow but then lost to Sweden. Since the organizers did not have the Swedish national anthem, the Swedish players sang a drinking song instead, which was played over the loudspeakers!

235. The Canadian ice hockey team was so strong that, in 1930, they did not play in the early rounds of the World Championships. The organizers put them directly in the final! The other teams played to see who would face Canada. Canada won 6-1 in the final and got the gold medal.

236. Slovakia once won a game against Bulgaria with a score of 82-0! This women's ice hockey match happened in Liepāja, Latvia, on September 6, 2008. It's now the world record for the biggest win ever in a senior international ice hockey game.

237. In 1950, most of the Soviet hockey team died in a plane crash. Vasily Stalin, the team's manager, and Stalin's son, hid the crash and replaced almost every player on the team to avoid his father's anger. Stalin never noticed the difference!

238. When a player scores a hat trick in a hockey game, and fans throw their hats onto the ice, they are either given to the player, thrown away, given to charity, or kept and shown off at the team's arena.

239. A company in Quebec named InGlasCo makes all the pucks for the NHL. They produce around 4 million pucks each year. On average, a puck used in the NHL lasts only 7 minutes before it's either lost to the stands or damaged!

240. An "apple" is slang for an assist.

241. In ice hockey, officials have 45 pucks ready for each game. That's 15 pucks for every period.

242. The US women's Olympic hockey team prepares for the Olympics by practicing against men's high school teams!

243. Almost 43% of active NHL players are from Canada! Only about 28% are from the US.

244. "Wheel" is slang for a player who can skate very fast and easily maneuver around the ice. It is often used as a compliment or an encouragement by teammates or coaches.

245. In 1980, after the famous "Miracle on Ice" hockey game, someone offered Boris Mikhailov, the captain of the USSR team, $1 million to leave Russia. Boris did not take the offer because KGB agents were next to him at that time.

246. Fox Sports once created a puck called FoxTrax that used augmented reality to create a blue glow around it when the game was seen on TV! The development of this puck cost $2 million. Each puck was $400. It was only used for two years, from 1996 to 1998.

247. NHL goalie Jonathan Bernier talked about Nelson Mandela after Mandela died. He called Mandela "a great guy off and on the ice" and "one of the most-known athletes."

248. Former NHL hockey player Miroslav Šatan has a name that sounds like "Satan," so people once made a joke on

April Fool's Day saying he was traded to the New Jersey Devils to be their captain, which would make Šatan the leader of the Devils.

249. In ice hockey, scoring three goals in a single game is called a hat trick. Fans often celebrate this by throwing hats onto the ice, a tradition that started in the 1950s. The origin of this custom is linked to various stories from Canadian cities where hatmakers would reportedly offer a free hat to players who achieved a hat trick!

250. In the National Hockey League (NHL), the word "National" refers to Canada.

251. During Vancouver Canucks hockey games at Rogers Arena, two fans known as the Green Men become famous within the crowd. The Green Men engage the crowd and distract opposing players with playful behavior, such as performing handstands against the glass and using various props.

252. The NHL has a rule that says if referees can't come to a game and no one else can replace them, the players must referee the game! This rule was used once on January 15, 1983, because a snowstorm stopped two of the three officials from getting to the game.

253. In the NHL, there are "emergency backup goalies" (EBUGs). If the main goalie and the second goalie get hurt in a game, the team can ask anyone in the arena to play as the goalie! The home team always has an amateur goalie ready, just in case.

254. Scott Foster, who at the time was a 36-year-old accountant, once played for the Chicago Blackhawks as an emergency goalie. It was his first NHL game. He stopped seven shots from the Winnipeg Jets and helped win the game!

255. Esa Tikkanen, a Finnish NHL player, was famous for speaking in a confusing way, which people called Tiki-Talk or Tikkanese. Wayne Gretzky once said, "He brings something special. I don't know what it is, but if you ask him, you couldn't understand his answer."

256. A "basket" is another word for the net, where you try to score a goal.

257. In 1977, the NHL made a rule that made it mandatory for players' names to be on jerseys. The Toronto Maple Leafs did not want to do this because they thought they would not sell as many game programs – that people often bought to check players' names. When the NHL said they would fine the team, the Maple Leafs wrote the names on the jerseys in the same color as the jersey so they couldn't be seen!

258. Paul Coffey, a famous NHL player, liked to wear very tight skates. So he chose skates that were two sizes too small on purpose!

259. Ted Lindsay, a legendary NHL player and Hall of Fame inductee, chose not to attend his induction ceremony because women weren't allowed there. His stand led the NHL to change its policy, allowing women into the ceremony the following year.

260. Most NHL players are born between January and June. This is because youth hockey players are grouped by their birth year. A player born in January is nearly a year older than one born in December, so they are bigger, which gives them an advantage and makes scouts more likely to choose them.

261. Goalie Normie Smith once lost 12 pounds (5,4 kg) by making 92 saves in an NHL playoff game!

262. When NHL player Jack Johnson became a pro, he gave his mother the power to manage his money. His parents then spent all of his money and lived in luxury. When he discovered this was happening, he tried to get agents and advisors to help with his money, but his mom fired them all!

263. The Ligue Nord-Américaine de Hockey (LNAH) is the world's toughest hockey league! It has an average of 3.2 fights per game. The NHL averages 0.6 fights per game.

264. "One on!" (or "two on" or "three on" or "man on") is a way of warning a teammate that an opponent is approaching them from behind or the side, and they need to act fast.

265. The Florida Panthers' "rat trick" is a hockey tradition
    that started when a player killed a rat with his stick and
    scored two goals in the same game. Fans began throwing
    plastic rats onto the ice to celebrate goals, reaching thou-
    sands of rats thrown during the 1996 Stanley Cup Finals!
    The NHL had to change the rules to penalize the home
    team for such disruptions.

266. Willie O'Ree was the first black man in the NHL and
    couldn't see with one eye! A puck hit his face when he

was 18 and made him blind in that eye. He kept it a secret during his whole 21-year hockey career!

267. The NHL has a rule named after a former player who tried to distract a goalie by waving his stick in front of his face during a playoff game in 2008. The rule, known as the "Sean Avery Rule," bans such behavior and imposes a two-minute penalty for offenders.

268. At age 14, Brendan Shanahan wanted hockey player Rick Vaive's autograph, but Vaive was rude and ignored him. After 4 years, Shanahan joined the NHL, and during his first game against Vaive, they fought, and Shanahan won the fight!

269. Wayne Gretzky's stats are so much better than other players' that if his career numbers were cut by half, he would still be among the greatest 20 players of all time!

270. Vinnie Paul from the band Pantera had a party where Guy Carbonneau, a Dallas Stars player, tried to toss the Stanley Cup from a balcony into a swimming pool. He missed, and the Stanley Cup hit the concrete instead, getting a dent! It later had to be fixed by silversmiths who work for the NHL.

271. Roger Nielson, a famous ice hockey coach, had an impressive skill for discovering and exploiting rule loopholes! Every time he would find a loophole, the NHL would have to change the rules so he couldn't use it anymore.

272. Roger Nielson found out that a hockey team couldn't have fewer than three players on the ice, even if they got a lot of penalties. So, once he was winning, he would start to purposely send too many players onto the ice. Because he kept breaking the rules, the referees had to stop the game. This meant the other team didn't get a chance to score. He would do this every 10 seconds until the time ran out.

273. Back then, the rules did not say you needed a goalie in the goal for a penalty shot. So, Roger Nielson would put a defenseman in place of the goalie. The rules also didn't say the goalie had to stay in the goal. So, when the other

team got ready for a penalty shot, the defenseman would run at them very fast and take the puck from them before they could take the penalty shot!

274. Roger Nielson was also the first coach to come up with the idea of practicing in the offseason. Before that, hockey teams didn't practice when the season was over!

275. Wayne Gretzky's most recent record was set after his retirement! He has an average of 1.921 points per game, which used to be the second-highest after Mario Lemieux, with an average of 2.005. But when Lemieux returned to playing hockey after retiring, his average went down! This made Gretzky move up to the first place.

276. The first outdoor game for the NHL happened in Las Vegas in September 1991. It was such a hot day that the temperature reached 95 °F (35 °C)!

277. Terry Sawchuk was an NHL goalie who got about 400 stitches on his face. He didn't wear a protective facemask until 1962. Life Magazine asked a make-up artist to show all of Sawchuk's injuries by putting fake stitches on his face. But the make-up artist ran out of space to show all of them!

278. "Cage" is slang for a type of face protection players wear on their helmets. It's made of wire and covers the whole face so that the puck, sticks, or anything else can't hit you in the face.

279. The New Jersey team in the NHL is named after the Jersey Devil. This is a legendary creature that some people say they've seen. Commodore Stephen Decatur and Joseph

Bonaparte, Napoleon's older brother, are two of those people. Decatur even tried to shoot it with a cannonball!

280. A big fight broke out during a hockey game in Piešťany, Slovakia, on January 4, 1987, that lasted for 20 minutes! To try to end it, the officials turned off the lights in the rink.

All the players in the fight were suspended for 18 months, but this was later cut down to 6 months. The coaches of both teams were suspended for three years.

281. The Pittsburgh Penguins had a monthly shootout contest when Dan Bylsma coached them. The player who didn't score a goal had to grow a mustache and was nicknamed 'Mustache Boy'!

282. Peter Taglianetti, a player in the NHL, once suffered a severe bruise on his ankle just after the first round of the Stanley Cup playoffs. To keep playing, he used a bag of peanut butter inside his skate to serve as a cushion!

283. Jarome Iginla, a hockey player, donated $2,000 to a charity called Kidsport every time he scored a goal. While playing, he donated over $700,000 to help children through this charity!

284. Billy Coutu was kicked out of the NHL because he attacked two referees in 1927! This happened after his team lost in the playoffs. Some people say his coach, Art Ross, told him to do it.

285. "Standing on his/her head" is slang for a goalie who is playing very well and making incredible saves.

286. The NHL does not own the Stanley Cup trophy. If there were to be a shutdown or a stop in NHL games because of disagreements, the actual owners of the trophy could give it to a team that is not part of the NHL!

287. Patrick Kaleta is such a big fan of LEGO blocks that he has a dedicated room just for his LEGO collection! He started playing with LEGO when he was healing from an injury.

288. Kris Draper earned the nickname "One Dollar Man" because he was traded for just one dollar in 1993! Later, he became one of only six players to play over 1,000 games for the Detroit Red Wings hockey team.

289. Darryl Sittler from the Toronto Maple Leafs holds the record for scoring the most points in one game. On February 7, 1976, he recorded 6 goals and 4 assists, 10 points in total!

290. In 1971, Bobby Orr became the first player to sign a contract worth a million dollars! The Boston Bruins agreed to pay him $200,000 yearly for five years. When you adjust for the rise in prices over time, known as inflation, $200k would be approximately $1,232,365 in today's currency.

291. The first goal in NHL history was scored on December 19, 1917. Dave Ritchie scored it while playing for the Montreal Wanderers in a game against the Toronto Arenas.

292. The first penalty shot in NHL history was taken by Art Ross. He later became a member of the Hockey Hall of Fame in 1949. The trophy for the top scorer in the NHL called the "Art Ross Trophy," is named after him.

293. A "garbage goal" or "picking up the trash" is slang for when a player scores a goal by quickly shooting the puck after it bounces off the goalie or the post. This is usually done from a very short distance, so the player does not have much time or space to aim.

294. On days when there was a game, Stephane Quintal would not speak to anyone after 1:30 in the afternoon! He would not respond to any attempts at conversation or answer any phone calls.

295. Stephan Labeau had a habit of chewing between 20 and 25 pieces of gum before each game! He made sure to spit the gum out precisely two minutes before the start of the game.

296. The longest shootout in NHL history had 20 rounds and happened on December 16, 2014. It was during a game between the Florida Panthers and the Washington Cap-

itals. The Florida Panthers won the game. They scored 6 goals out of their 20 chances in the shootout. The Washington Capitals scored only 5 goals and lost the game.

297. During the Summit Series, NHL All-Star player Phil Esposito discovered a screw on the floor and thought it was a spying device planted by the Soviets. To stop them from listening in, he removed the screw, but it turned out it was actually holding up a crystal chandelier in the room below, which crashed to the ground when the screw was removed!

298. In 1929, professional ice hockey player Eddie Shore was determined to get to a game after he missed his train. Despite a severe snowstorm, he drove 350 miles to reach the game!

On the way, the chains on the tires broke two times, the windshield wipers stopped working so he had to take off the top part of the windshield; and he also had an accident and his car ended up in a ditch. He still arrived at the game on time, played, and even scored the match's only goal!

299. In 2010, during a hockey playoff game between the Sharks and the Red Wings, a fan of the Sharks team tossed a three-foot (91 cm) real leopard shark onto the ice rink with an octopus in its mouth!

300. In December 1990, Paul Cavallini had his fingertip cut off when he stopped a slapshot with his hand! He could not play for 13 games because of the injury.

301. Jay Beagle has achieved the unique feat of winning championships in three major hockey leagues: the National Hockey League (NHL), the American Hockey League (AHL), and the ECHL (formerly the East Coast Hockey League). He was the first player to accomplish this!

302. Wayne Gretzky had a habit of tucking in the right side of his shirt. He began doing this when he was only six years old and played hockey with older kids who were ten. Since Wayne was smaller and the team shirts were too large for him, he tucked in the right side to stop the shirt from interfering with his ability to control the puck. This tucking in became his signature style throughout his career.

303. Swedish hockey player Peter Forsberg, who won the Stanley Cup twice with the Colorado Avalanche, earned more money in Sweden by investing in the popular shoe brand 'Crocs' than in his NHL career!

304. In 2002, during the Salt Lake City Olympics, professional ice hockey player Jarome Iginla started talking with four fans near his table. He learned they were sleeping in their car because they didn't have a place to stay. Jarome Iginla quietly arranged for them to have a room at the hotel where his family was staying, and he paid for it himself.

305. The U.S. military gives money to professional sports teams for them to show patriotism. During the years 2012 to 2014, they spent $10.4 million on deals with teams in the NHL (hockey), NFL (football), MLB (baseball), NBA (basketball), and MLS (soccer) for this purpose.

306. NHL ice hockey rinks are smaller than those used in the Olympics or international competitions. The size comes

from the first ice hockey rink, the Victoria Skating Rink in Montreal, Canada.

307. When a player sprays ice on the goalie by stopping quickly in front of them, it's called "snowing the goalie," and this action can lead to a minor penalty in ice hockey.

308. As a child, winger Tie Domi admired Bobby Clarke so much that he decided he wanted to have Clarke's iconic toothless grin. So, he went outside and threw his head against the handlebars of his bike, knocking out his front teeth. And after his adult teeth grew in, he did it again!

309. Nathan Horton is the only player to have scored a point in a game he didn't play. In 2014, Horton scored a goal for the Columbus Blue Jackets during a match against the Dallas Stars. The goal came about four minutes before the game was stopped and postponed because another player

had a medical emergency. When they played the game again, Horton couldn't play in the new game because he was hurt, but the Blue Jackets began with a 1-0 lead thanks to Horton's earlier goal!

310. In 2004, researchers at Stanford Graduate School of Business discovered that NHL fans were the best-educated compared to fans of the other three major sports leagues! They also found that NHL fans often bought more season tickets because they usually had more money.

311. Wayne Gretzky did not complete his high school education!

312. Hockey is the reason airplanes exist! Wilbur Wright, one of the brothers who invented the airplane, got hurt while playing hockey; the injury made him lose some teeth, and it took a long time for him to recover. Because of this, he decided not to go to Yale University as planned, and instead, he joined his brother Orville in running their business, changing history forever!

313. Some people have made jokes about Ice Hockey being nothing more than a long con because Jack Gibson, who founded the first professional hockey league, was also a dentist!

314. Barack Obama once referred to hockey player Brad Marchand as a "little ball of hate"!

315. Paris Hilton was a hockey player during her high school years!

316. Every time the U.S. men's hockey team won a gold medal at the Olympics, the team had at least one player from

the small town of Warroad in Minnesota, which has a population of only around 1,700 people!

317. In 1928, the Stanley Cup was stored in Lester Patrick's basement. Lester Patrick's young boys used a hammer and nail to scratch their names onto the trophy. Years later, in 1940, both sons won the Stanley Cup while playing for the New York Rangers. After their win, their names were officially engraved on the cup!

318. The Minnesota Wild hockey team has officially retired the number 1 jersey because their fans are number 1!

319. Ariana Grande was hit by hockey pucks twice before she turned 6 years old. Both times, it happened during NHL games. She was also the first person ever to get hit by a puck at the Florida Panthers' new arena!

320. A "pizza" is slang for a terrible pass that goes through the center of the ice, where it is easy for the other team to steal it. It's like giving them a free pizza because they don't have to work hard to get it.

321. Jarome Iginla, a Canadian right winger, was the first black man to earn a gold medal in the Winter Olympic Games!

322. "Icing" is a move where a player sends the puck to the other end of the rink on purpose to keep it far from their own goal. The Boston Bruins once did this 87 times in one game because they were unhappy that there was no rule against it. It took the hockey league five more years before they made a rule about icing.

323. Some people believe the first-ever "crowd wave" happened without planning at an NHL ice hockey game! In 1980, Colorado Rockies fans started standing up in their seats a bit later than the people next to them. This created a wave that went all around the arena, and it was the first time this was ever recorded at any sports event!

324. Steve Carell, known for his role as Michael Scott in The Office, played hockey as a kid! He was a goalie, and his team actually won a national championship!

325. Before the Coyotes hockey team moved to Glendale, they played in a place with only 10,923 seats. But over two years, they sold an average of 13,179 tickets for each game!

326. A "bottle rocket" is when a player shoots the puck so hard and perfectly that it flies into the goal and hits the water bottle that the goalies usually keep on top of the net.

327. In 1992, the Edmonton Oilers traded Bruce Bell, who plays defense, for goalie Kari Takko from the Minnesota North Stars. People made a joke about the trade by calling it the "Takko-Bell" trade because it sounded like the name of the famous fast food place, Taco Bell.

328. For 21 seasons, from 1980 to 2001, only 3 players won the Art Ross Trophy. Wayne Gretzky won it 10 times, Mario Lemieux won it 6 times, and Jaromir Jagr won it 5 times! The Art Ross Trophy is given yearly to the NHL player who scores the most points during the regular season.

329. Henri Richard had 10 out of his 11 Stanley Cup rings stolen. Despite the thieves asking for money to return them, Richard refused to pay!

330. About 63% of parents with kids who play hockey say they didn't play hockey themselves when they were young.

331. In Finland, the top-scoring player on each ice hockey team gets to wear a special shiny gold helmet!

332. Brooks Orpik only scored 18 goals across the 1,035 games he played in his career!

333. Wayne Gretzky once played a game for the New York Rangers while wearing a jersey with a misspelled nameplate! It was spelled "Gretkzy" instead of "Gretzky".

334. Wayne Gretzky almost joined the Winnipeg Jets, but the team's general manager decided at the last moment not to sign him. He thought Gretzky was too skinny to be successful in the NHL!

335. Hockey player Sam LoPresti was once lost in the sea for 42 days! LoPresti served on a ship during World War II. The ship was hit by a torpedo and sunk, and he was initially thought to have been killed. But he survived on a lifeboat along with 26 other men for 42 days with little food or water before being rescued near Brazil. He even caught a dolphin, which helped feed and keep everyone alive!

336. The IIHF (International Ice Hockey Federation) World Women's Championship has taken place 22 times. In all of these except for one, the final match for the gold medal was between Canada and the USA!

337. During a pre-Olympics exhibition game in 1980, when the US played against the USSR, people discovered a Soviet player had a hidden gun under his jersey! This person was actually a KGB agent, there to stop players from escaping to the West.

338. The first time the USSR played against the NHL, they didn't know much about American hockey or the US because they had been so isolated. Their hockey style was very different at the time, with less physical contact. During the first game with the NHL, the Russians noticed many players were missing teeth. This made them think that there were no dentists in America!

339. Mike Emrick, a commentator for NHL games, is called "Doc" because he completed a PhD in film and television at Bowling Green State University!

340. Zdeno Chara, a Slovak defenceman, knows how to speak seven different languages: Slovak, Czech, Polish, Swedish, Russian, German, and English!

341. When Zdeno Chara was the leader of the Bruins hockey team, he didn't allow people to use the word "rookie." This was because, in his early days in Trencin, new players had to do demeaning rituals or chores. He promised himself that he wouldn't let this happen to others if he was ever in charge. So, in the Bruins' changing room, new players are called "first-year players," "younger guys," or "newer guys" in a respectful way.

342. Before the 1960s, it was common for TV broadcasts of NHL games to start only during the second period! They did this to encourage fans to buy tickets to watch the game in person at the arena and because they believed most people would only watch TV later in the evening anyway.

343. The logo on the Montreal Canadiens hockey team's jerseys shows "NHL" when they play in other cities, and it shows "LNH," which stands for NHL in French when they play at their own arena!

344. The Florida Panthers' team has different designs for their jerseys. When they play in their own stadium, their outfits have the word "Panthers" on them. But, when they play games in other places, their outfits say "Florida" instead.

345. The Penguins hold the records for the most consecutive wins and the most consecutive losses in NHL history!

346. Before 2015, pro female hockey players didn't earn a salary for playing.

347. Sidney Crosby averages 108 points per 82-game season, making him one of the best players of all time!

348. Renowned writer Hunter S. Thompson wrote two articles about hockey player Patrick Roy for ESPN!

349. Wayne Gretzky was the top player in assists in the NHL during 16 out of his 20 seasons!

350. Right winger Phil Kessel also plays in the World Series of Poker and has won more than $17,000 during his poker career!

351. Defenseman Chris Chelios has a younger cousin named Chris Chelios, who also played hockey!

352. Even though they were both born in the US, Nick Foligno plays for the USA team, and his brother Marcus Foligno plays for the Canada team.

353. When two hockey players have the same points at the end of the season, the one who gets the Art Ross Trophy is decided by tiebreaker rules. The third rule is that the trophy goes to the player who scored the earliest goal in that season.

354. The Soviet Union trained real bears to play ice hockey! The Moscow Circus on Ice, which started in 1962, included bears that played ice hockey. A 1970 article from New York Magazine mentioned that these bears played hockey at the Felt Forum in Madison Square Garden. There are still videos online of bears playing ice hockey!

355. Patrick Kane is the only player from the US who has ever won the Art Ross Trophy! He achieved this in 2016.

356. Stan Mikita is the only ice hockey player ever to win three top awards in the NHL in the same year. These awards are the Art Ross Trophy for scoring the most points, the Hart Trophy for being the most valuable player, and the Lady Byng Trophy for showing good behavior and sportsmanship. He achieved this remarkable feat two times!

357. Ice hockey pucks are kept in a freezer in the penalty box and replaced before every period.

358. In 2007, Sidney Crosby, at just 19 years old, became the youngest person ever to win the Art Ross Trophy. No one as young as Crosby has ever been the top scorer in a big professional sports league in North America before him!

359. In 1979, Guy Lafleur, who played for the Montreal Canadiens, made a music album giving hockey tips over disco music!

360. Chris Drury is the only individual who has achieved the unique feat of winning both a Stanley Cup in hockey and a Little League World Series in baseball!

361. Referee Paul Devorski's mom worked as a nurse and helped deliver Logan Couture when he was born. She was in the room during his birth!

362. Kaapo Kakko is a hockey player with two health conditions: Type 1 diabetes, which means his body doesn't produce enough insulin, and Celiac Disease, which means he can't eat gluten because it harms his intestines.

363. Frederik Andersen is the first professional ice hockey goalie from Denmark to play in the NHL!

364. The investment firm Bain Capital once attempted to buy the entire NHL for $4 billion!

365. Brandon Prust sends his hockey sticks back home to his former junior coach so he can rub them and bring him good luck!

366. San Jose Sharks' mascot, Sharkie, once helped Steve Harwell, the lead singer of Smash Mouth, eat 24 eggs! In 2011, at an event in California, with chef Guy Fieri cooking the eggs, Harwell ate the eggs with help from the crowd, raising $15,000 for charity!

367. The movie "Elf" with actor Will Ferrell had a hockey scene that was deleted!

368. From 2006 to 2012, Dominic Moore played for nine different NHL teams!

369. Mario Lemieux and Patrick Roy share the same birthday!

370. Terry Sawchuk holds the record for the most career ties in hockey with 172!

371. Before the 1987 Canada Cup, Wayne Gretzky invited players from the Soviet team, along with their KGB agents, to a barbecue at his house!

372. Ivan Boldirev got his name on the Stanley Cup before ever playing in an NHL game! After becoming a professional hockey player in 1969, he played for a minor league team in Oklahoma City. He was added to the Boston Bruins' team during the 1970 playoffs but didn't play. Still, Boston won the championship, and Boldirev's name was put on the Cup.

373. In 1967, the Toronto Maple Leafs won the Stanley Cup, and they included the name of the person who dressed up as their team mascot on the trophy!

374. When the Latvian ice hockey team wins a game at home, fans go to the opposing team's embassy and put flowers at the gate!

375. The Montréal Canadiens really wanted Jean Béliveau to play for them, but he did not want to leave his amateur team in Québec. To get him to join, the Canadiens purchased his entire amateur league!

376. Fighting has been common in ice hockey since the sport
    became popular. This could be because there weren't
    many rules when ice hockey was invented, so players
    often used force to control the game. Some people also
    think it's because there were a lot of poor people and
    crime in Canada during the 1800s.

377. Tiger Williams holds the record for the most penalty
    minutes ever in the NHL. He spent around 2.7 days sitting
    in the penalty box during his hockey career!

378. There's an extreme sport called underwater ice hockey, where players play upside-down under a layer of ice in frozen ponds or pools, using a puck that floats! They wear masks to see, fins to swim, and special suits to stay warm. They don't carry air tanks and have to come up for air about every 30 seconds.

379. Helmuts Balderis is the oldest person to be drafted into the NHL at 36 years of age. The Minnesota team chose him in 1989, even though he had not played for five years. He appeared in 26 games, scoring 3 goals and 6 assists.

380. Russian hockey player Slava Fetisov, known as one of the greatest defensemen of all time, never lost a game from when he was 6 until he turned 18. He was undefeated for 240 consecutive games!

381. Being struck by a slapshot in hockey that's moving at 100 miles per hour (160 km/h) has the same force as being hit by a bullet from a .38 S&W handgun fired from 100 yards away (91 m).

382. Goaltender Georges Vezina was known as "The Chicoutimi Cucumber" because he was always calm, even when playing high-pressure games.

383. Matt Murray achieved the impressive feat of winning the Stanley Cup twice as a rookie!

384. Bill Mosienko set an impressive record by scoring three goals, known as a hat trick, in just 21 seconds during a hockey game!

385. Wayne Gretzky's first professional goal was scored against the Edmonton Oilers! At the time, he was playing for the Indianapolis Racers in a league known as the WHA. Later, Wayne Gretzky joined the Oilers, which eventually became part of the NHL.

386. Three out of every four goals Derrick Pouliot scored during his career were game-winners!

387. Every time Chris Pronger was traded from a team during his career, that team failed to reach the playoffs in the next season!

388. A "fishbowl" is a type of protective face mask that hockey players wear. It's called a "fishbowl" because it's made of clear plastic and covers the whole face.

389. Wayne Gretzky was so strong that many Fantasy Hockey leagues had to separate his stats into two players: Gretzky (Goals) and Gretzky (Assists)!

390. Red Kelly, a Hall of Famer, won 2 of his 8 Stanley Cups while also a Canadian Member of Parliament!

391. Stan Mikita used to be one of the players that got the most penalties in hockey, but he changed his behavior and won the Lady Byng Trophy twice, for sportsmanship and gentlemanly conduct combined with excellence, after his daughter asked, "Mommy, why does Daddy spend so much time sitting down [in the penalty box]?"

392. In 1349, King Edward III of England made playing football and hockey illegal because he wanted more people to practice archery instead! Archery was very important for battles during that time.

393. Jaromir Jagr wears the number 68 on his jersey to honor his grandfather. His grandfather died in 1968 when people in Czechoslovakia protested against Soviet control in an event called the Prague Spring.

394. Some records show that the slapshot was created in Nova Scotia by Eddie Martin, an African-Canadian player, in 1906. This was 11 years before the creation of the NHL.

395. In 2014, for the Olympic hockey final where Canada played for the gold medal, the government allowed bars to open early at 4:30 in the morning so people could watch the game.

396. The band Coldplay sponsors a small Swedish hockey team! Guy Berryman is the bass player for Coldplay. His brother, Mark Berryman, lives in Sweden and has persuaded Coldplay to provide equipment and clothes for a young hockey team in Sweden called Säters IF.

397. The NASA Jet Propulsion Laboratory has a recreational hockey team named the Rovers!

398. Darryl Sittler once set a record by scoring 10 points in one game. The night he did this, he had a different meal before the game than usual because he was busy with errands. He ate chicken and fries from Swiss Chalet!

399. Mike Milbury, who played for the Boston Bruins, once got so angry with an unruly fan that he jumped over the glass, tore off the fan's shoe, and beat him with it! He was not allowed to play for six games because of this, and afterward, all hockey rinks got taller glass barriers to prevent this from happening again.

400. Coach Roger Nielson once learned about a rule that says you can take your goalie out and put another player in to skate. So, he would do it and ask the goalie to leave his stick in front of the net when he left the ice. And the stick would just lie there, blocking the goal! At that time, no rules stopped you from doing this! A new rule had to be invented to stop goalies from leaving anything blocking the net.

401. There is a prize called the Viking Award that goes to the person who is considered the season's best Swedish ice hockey player in North America and is voted for by the players themselves.

402. In Sweden, there was an unusual incident where a hockey player found the puck stuck in his pants during a game. He managed to glide behind the opposing team's goalie and into the goal area. He squatted and dropped the puck from his pants into the net. Surprisingly, the officials decided the goal was valid and allowed it to count!

403. Since its inception in 1972, the Hart Trophy, given to the most valuable player in the NHL, has been won by a defenseman just once! Chris Pronger was the player who achieved this in 2000.

404. Grant Fuhr, a goalie, made 14 assists in the 1983-1984 hockey season. He is the only goalie in history to get over 10 points in one season!

405. Dave Grohl, the founder and lead singer of the rock band Foo Fighters, considered goalie Jim Craig one of his personal heroes. In 1980, when the U.S. Olympic hockey team beat Russia, Grohl found the phone numbers of all the Jim Craigs in that area and called them so he could reach Craig and congratulate him personally!

406. Musician Michael Bublé is a big hockey fan! When he goes on tour, one of the items on the list of things he needs for his performance is a hockey puck from the local hockey team.

407. Famous hockey player Jaromir Jagr has a big problem with gambling. He has lost so much money that he even had to go into debt for $500,000. A bookie once said, "The guy lost just about every bet he ever made with us."

408. Even though ice hockey is one of the most popular sports in North America, field hockey is actually much more popular in the rest of the world, with around 2 billion fans! This makes it the 3rd most popular sport globally, after soccer (football) and cricket!

409. Scott Niedermayer is the only hockey player who has won every possible North American and international Championship in his career! He has won a Gold Medal at the IIHF World Junior Championship, the Memorial Cup in the WHL, four Stanley Cups, two Olympic Gold Medals, and Gold at both the World Championships and the World Cup of Hockey.

410. "One-Eyed" Frank McGee, a hockey player who lost vision in one eye because of a hockey injury, cheated on the vision test required to join the military during WWI! When the medical officer asked him to cover one eye at a time and read from a chart, he just switched hands and covered the same eye, tricking the doctor!

411. The famous hockey player Maurice Richard switched his jersey number from 15 to 9 to celebrate his first child, a baby girl who was born weighing 9 pounds.

412. A sports journalist once asked Borje Salming, the leader of the Swedish hockey team, why his team wasn't doing well. He replied, "Too many Swedes."

413. In the 2010 Olympic Hockey Final, the airline Air Canada had to postpone a flight because the passengers refused to get on the plane until the game had finished!

414. Jerome Iginla, a former Canadian professional ice hockey winger, has an unusually long name! His full name is Jarome Arthur-Leigh Adekunle Tig Junior Elvis Iginla.

415. The record for the most players playing in an ice hockey exhibition game is 433! This event happened in Canada in 2016. The game had two teams, Black and Red, with Black winning 84 to 69. The match lasted for 7 hours and 5 minutes.

416. Alice Beretta from Italy scored the quickest goal in women's ice hockey, just 1 second after the game started! The match took place in Switzerland on December 14, 2013.

417. The largest ice hockey tournament ever held was Calgary,
     Canada's 37th Minor Hockey Week. It happened from
     January 5 to January 13, 2007. In this tournament, there
     were 664 teams with 10,922 players in total! Throughout
     the week, they played 957 games. Also, 2,694 coaches and
     450 referees took part in this big event.

418. In January 2010, during an away game in Vancouver, a
     fan of the Canucks team kept pointing a laser at the eyes
     of Miikka Kiprusoff, the goalie for the visiting team, the
     Flames, the whole time he was playing!

419. The most people ever to attend an ice hockey game was 104,173! The game occurred at the Michigan Football Stadium in the United States in Ann Arbor, Michigan, on December 11, 2010.

420. In 1930, a hockey puck struck a pack of matches in goalie Abie Goldberry's pocket, which set him on fire! People quickly extinguished the flames, and although Goldberry was hurt, he survived the incident.

421. Zdeno Chara from Slovakia, who played for the Boston Bruins, hit the hardest shot ever in the NHL. He did this at a Skills Competition in the All-Star Game. His slapshot speed was 108.8 miles per hour (175.5 km/h)!

422. The longest contract ever signed in NHL history is for 15 years. Rick DiPietro (USA) signed this contract with the New York Islanders in 2006. His contract was worth $67.5 million. Later, Ilya Kovalchuk (Russia) also signed a 15-year contract, this time with the New Jersey Devils, in 2010, worth $100 million.

423. Glenn Hall, a hockey goalkeeper, played in an impressive 502 games in a row, from 1952 to 1971. This set a record for the most consecutive games played by a goalie!

424. A team from Canada in the NHL is named after an event from the US Civil War. The team is called the Calgary Flames. They were originally the Atlanta Flames, a name that referred to General Sherman's burning of the city of Atlanta in the Civil War.

425. The draft order was once decided by how teams finished in the season, with the last-place team picking first. But in 1993, the Ottawa Senators purposely lost games to come in last and get the top draft pick. Because of this, the draft lottery was created to prevent teams from losing on purpose to get a better draft position.

426. In 1975, the Chicago Blackhawks hockey team played a game against Sesame Street around Christmas time! The Cookie Monster was a goalkeeper during the game and ate a puck!

427. In 1983, Tom Martin, a player in the American Hockey League known as "Bussey," became the only hockey player in history to be traded in exchange for a bus!

Unfortunately, he never got to see the bus because authorities took it away at the border between Canada and the United States soon after the trade took place.

428. Actor Will Smith is a part owner of the New Jersey Devils hockey team!

429. Sidney Crosby has won an Emmy Award! He won it in 2016 for his role in "There's No Place Like Home With Sidney Crosby."

430. The Penguins and Predators use exactly the same yellow color on their logos and uniforms. The specific name of the color is Pantone 1235C.

431. The name of the NHL team, the Winnipeg Jets, comes directly from the NFL team called the New York Jets!

432. The St. Louis Blues hockey team has fired four of the most successful coaches of all time! These coaches are Scotty Bowman, Joel Quenneville, Ken Hitchcock, and Al Arbour.

433. No one invited coach John Tortorella to the after-party when his team, the Tampa Bay Lightning, won the 2004 Stanley Cup!

434. "Saucy paws," "silky mitts," or "soft hands" is slang for a player who can handle the puck smoothly and make

quick and precise passes or shots. They're a joy to watch and a nightmare to defend against.

435. Carey Price's father bought him an airplane to fly to hockey practice because it was about 200 miles (320 km) away from their home! Using the plane reduced the journey to only 45 minutes.

436. The Pittsburgh Penguins hockey team used to have a real penguin named Pete as their team mascot! Pete showed up for the first time at a game between the Penguins and the Bruins on October 19, 1968, during a break in the middle of the game. Sadly, Pete died shortly after, about a month into the hockey season. People think he died because the place he lived in wasn't cold enough. After Pete died, the Penguins got another penguin to be their mascot, and this one stayed with them until the hockey season finished in 1972!

437. Daniel Brière is unique in NHL history as the first player to have his name on his jersey with an accent mark.

438. Former goaltender José Théodore's father's name is Theodore. His name is Theodore Théodore!

439. When a team takes out their goalie during overtime, and then the other team scores a goal into the empty net, the team that removed their goalie doesn't get the extra point they would have earned for making it into overtime.

440. A "suicide pass" or "suey" is a pass that puts the receiver in a dangerous position, usually exposing them to a hard hit from an opponent.

441. Matt Doherty, who acted as Les Averman in the Mighty Ducks movies, couldn't skate or play hockey when he first got the role. But, by the time they made the third movie, he had become so good that he led his high school hockey team as its captain and even got an offer for a scholarship to play hockey in college!

442. Over 26.5 million Canadians watched the men's hockey final in the 2010 Winter Olympics. That is 80% of the country's population!

443. The NBA was started to help ice hockey arenas earn extra money! Back in June 1946, in New York City, Walter Brown, who owned the Boston Garden, saw that the ice hockey arenas were empty often. He decided to fill them up by having basketball games and created the Basketball Association of America. Three years later, in 1949, it joined forces with another league called the National Basketball League, and that's how the NBA was born.

444. Older hockey rinks used to have a single penalty box where players from opposing teams sat together. This often led to them fighting even while serving penalty time!

445. In 1905, a member of the Ottawa Senators tried and failed to dropkick the Stanley Cup across the Rideau Canal! The cup was left in the canal until it was retrieved the next day.

446. Maurice "Rocket" Richard, an ice hockey legend, chipped his front teeth in 1957 while drinking from the Stanley Cup!

447. Back in 1964, Red Kelly from the Toronto Maple Leafs had a funny moment when his baby son took a pee in the Stanley Cup during a photo shoot! After that, Red Kelly always found it hilarious whenever he saw other players taking a drink from the Cup.

448. Bryan Trottier of the New York Islanders once slept with the Stanley Cup in his bed, and it turns out that many players have done the same!

449. The famous goalie Martin Brodeur ate popcorn right out of the Stanley Cup. It was so messy that it left butter stains and salt damage inside the Cup for eight days until his teammate Jamie Langenbrunner cleaned it up.

450. Just a week after the Detroit team won the Stanley Cup, Kris Draper's newborn daughter had a little accident and pooped in the Cup while sitting in it. But they cleaned it very well, and Kris Draper even took a drink from the Cup on the same day!

451. A type of wasp from Kenya has been named after Tuukka Rask, a skilled ice hockey goalie from Finland who plays for the Boston Bruins. The official scientific name for this wasp is *Thaumatodryinus tuukkaraski*!

452. The Storhamar Dragons and Sparta Warriors, two Norwegian ice hockey teams, played the world's longest professional game. It lasted 217 minutes and 14 seconds, or 3 hours and 37 minutes, included eight rounds of overtime, and took eight hours to finish!

453. Zach Lamppa made the longest ice hockey pass ever: 904.33 feet (275.63 meters) to Tom Chorske. They did this on Lake of the Isles in Minneapolis.

454. In 1924, the Montreal Canadiens had a flat tire on their car while heading to their celebration for winning the championship. They took out the Stanley Cup from the car's trunk so they could repair the tire. And then they accidentally left the trophy on the side of the road! Fortunately, it was still there when they remembered and returned for it.

455. Brett Hull was banned from the Blackhawks' locker room as a kid. He got into trouble for using the equipment manager's hacksaw to cut everything he found!

456. Players often tape their hockey sticks to improve grip, control, and to protect the stick from damage. Patterns and styles of taping can vary by player preference, with some covering the entire blade while others only tape certain parts.

457. Turk Broda struggled with weight gain so often that his contract had a clause about weight! He was supposed to be 5'9 and 165 pounds (175 cm and 75 kg). But he often played at a weight up to 40 pounds heavier (18 kg). Every payday, Turk had to weigh himself. He got a bonus if he was less than 190 pounds (86 kg). If he was over 190 pounds, he lost some of his pay!

458. Brad Marchand and Torey Krug were known for their holiday costume parties!

459. In the fast-paced sport of ice hockey, known as one of the fastest games in the world, players typically only stay on the ice for an average of 47 seconds during each shift before switching out with teammates.

460. Wayne Gretzky holds an incredible record in ice hockey—he occupies nine out of the top eleven spots for the most points scored in a single NHL season! 1st, 2nd, 3rd, 4th, 6th, 7th, 9th, 10th, and 11th!

461. In the history of the NHL, only three players have ever achieved over 100 assists in a single season. These players were Bobby Orr and Mario Lemieux, who each accomplished it once, and Wayne Gretzky, who did it 11 seasons in a row!

462. Wayne Gretzky and his brother Brent Gretzky hold the NHL record for the most combined points scored by two brothers, totaling 2,861! Wayne scored 2,857, and Brent scored 4.

463. During a meeting with fans in Ottawa, Chris Wideman shared with some children that his favorite Christmas moment was when he told his little sister, who was 6 years old then, that Santa Claus is not real! As punishment for telling her this, he had to wear an elf costume every time he went to the ice hockey rink for two weeks!

464. The Columbus Blue Jackets have a cannon and fire it each time they score a goal during a game!

465. In ice hockey, a player earns a "point" by scoring a goal or helping another player score a goal, known as an assist. Wayne Gretzky holds the record for the most points in history. But Gretzky has so many assists (1,963) that even if he had never scored any goals, he would still have the most points of any player ever!

466. A "lip sweater" is slang for a mustache.

467. Sidney Crosby is famous for having a lot of superstitions. These included not talking to his mom on the day of a game, raising his feet and touching the window when his team's bus crossed train tracks, making sure no one touched his hockey sticks after he taped them (he would retape them if someone did), avoiding walking past the opposing team's locker room, eating a peanut butter and jelly sandwich at 5 pm, and always wearing the same protective cup!

468. "Kronwalled" is a term used to describe a big and powerful body check by a defender on an opposing player. It comes from the name of Niklas Kronwall, a former Swedish hockey player who played for the Detroit Red Wings and was known for his hard-hitting style.

469. The National Hockey League (NHL) was created because many team owners in the National Hockey Association (NHA) had problems with Eddie Livingstone, who owned the Toronto Blueshirts. They didn't like the way he did business. The rules of the NHA wouldn't let them ban him, so they created a new league, the NHL. This left Eddie Livingstone and his team as the only team left in the NHA!

470. The Masterton Trophy is given to the ice hockey player who "best exemplifies the qualities of perseverance, sportsmanship, and dedication to ice hockey.". This trophy is named in honor of Bill Masterton, who is sadly known for being the only player in the National Hockey League (NHL) to have passed away because of injuries he suffered during a match.

471. Keanu Reeves, famous for his roles in action films such as "The Matrix" and "John Wick," was once known for being an outstanding hockey goalie. People called him "The Wall". His skills as a goalie even got him a chance to try out for a team called the Windsor Spitfires, which plays in the Ontario Hockey League!

472. Justin Bieber loves to play hockey! In 2017, he participated in the NHL All-Star game, where he showed his hockey skills and even shared videos of him scoring goals on Instagram!

473. In Canada, even though most hockey players are naturally right-handed, about 70% of them prefer to play with sticks made for the left hand. In contrast, 70% of hockey players in the United States choose sticks designed for right-handed use.

474. Art Ross, whose name is on the trophy awarded to the player with the most points in a season, scored just 1 point in his entire NHL career!

475. Hockey players outside the US who play in the NHL and wish to live in the US after they stop playing need to prove they have "extraordinary" skills. For example, becoming an all-star or having won the Stanley Cup.

476. TJ Oshie's nickname has an interesting story. The "J" in his nickname actually doesn't mean anything! His real first name is Timothy. The reason he's called TJ is because his mom once saw a movie called "The Champ," and there was a young boy named TJ in it. She liked that name and decided her son should be called TJ, too!

477. Ebbie Goodfellow, a Canadian professional player and coach, was once fined $50 because he stuck his tongue out at a referee!

478. Hockey player Ed Belfour, who played as a goalie in the NHL, once tried to bribe Dallas police with 1 billion dollars to let him go after they arrested him!

479. Former hockey player Nicklas Grossmann's last name was spelled wrong on his shirt for over five years because he was too shy to tell anyone to correct it!

480. In 1996, hockey player Andy Bezeau from the International Hockey League was traded for "considerations," meaning something that would be decided later. That something turned out to be two equipment dryers!

481. Georges Laraque, who used to play in the NHL, decided to become vegan after he saw the documentary Earthlings. After that, he became the narrator for the French version of the film!

482. In 2015, Zemgus Girgensons, a hockey player in the NHL, received the most votes to play in the All-Star game, totaling 1,574,896 votes. Most of these votes, about 1,200,000, were from people in Latvia, where he is from, even though Latvia's population is just 1,997,500 people!

483. Anders Lee is the only NHL player who has his first name, Anders, on his jersey instead of his last name.

484. Referees and team coaches come together before a game, after it ends, and the following day, to talk about the decisions the referees made or didn't make during the game. These discussions help them understand the calls and address any issues or questions the coaches might have.

485. The record for the longest non-professional game of ice hockey played is 261 hours and 15 seconds! A Canadian organization called Hockey Marathon for the Kids set this record from March 31 to April 11, 2022, to raise money for charity. They collected $850,000 during the event to help the Alberta Children's Hospital Foundation.

486. In 1981, famous hockey player Wayne Gretzky appeared as a guest on the TV soap opera "The Young and the Restless." He was a big fan of soap operas at the time. During his appearance, he played the role of a mafia boss from Edmonton, and his only line was, "Call me Wayne, everybody does."

487. During the 2014 Olympic hockey game between the USA and Canada, broadcaster Doc Emrick used 153 different verbs to describe how the puck was moving!

488. Wayne Gretzky's wife once had an accident at Madison Square Garden when a piece of clear, hard plastic fell and hit her, making her pass out. Even though she was hurt and unconscious, Gretzky decided to finish playing the game instead of going with her to the hospital.

489. Drake, the famous Canadian rapper and singer, briefly appeared in an Indian-Canadian hockey comedy movie called Breakaway, which was released in English and Punjabi.

490. Adam Sherlip and The Hockey Foundation from the USA played the highest altitude game ever, at 14,307 feet (4,361 meters)! They did this in Chibra Kargyam, India.

491. Derek MacKay from Canada set a record by wearing 37 ice hockey jerseys at the same time!

492. Slovakia set the record for the highest score in an international ice hockey match by beating Bulgaria 82-0! This happened during a women's pre-Olympic qualification game in Liepaja, Latvia, on September 6, 2008.

493. Per Olsen scored the fastest goal in professional men's ice hockey history. He did it 2 seconds into the match! This happened during a game between Rungsted and Odense in Denmark's First Division.

494. Many goalies have a superstition that makes them avoid
stepping on the ice lines, believing it brings bad luck.
Especially the blue and crease lines – during play or when
they enter the ice.

495. In 1993, at a Jets hockey game in Canada, each person
got a sample jar of peanut butter. The fans were so angry
when the team lost the game after being ahead that they
threw hundreds of peanut butter jars onto the ice!

496. Jaromir Jagr had a unique ritual where he was always the last player to leave the ice after warm-ups, believing it gave him extra focus and luck for the game.

497. The 1974-75 Washington Capitals were probably the worst team ever in the NHL. When they beat the Pittsburgh Penguins 8-4 in their last game that year, it was their 8th win. They celebrated by holding up a trash can like it was the Stanley Cup and celebrating in the locker room!

498. There's a hockey team of Canadian priests called the Flying Fathers. They travel around North America and play games to raise money for different charities. The team's motto is "praying and playing," and they use two horses named Patience and Penance as backup goalies!

499. Before every home game, Alex Ovechkin eats at Mamma Luccia's. He always orders the Ovi Special, a big meal with chicken parmesan, noodles, bread, and cheese.

500. At the 2002 Salt Lake City Olympics, a Canadian icemaker named Trent Evans hid a "lucky loonie" under the ice (a nickname for the Canadian 1-dollar coin). He put the coin in the middle of the hockey rink and left it there as a hidden good luck charm for Canada's hockey teams. The men's and women's teams both won gold medals, with the men's team winning for the first time in 50 years! The loonie was later taken out and given to the Hockey Hall of Fame in Toronto.

501. In 1907, following a photo session, the Montreal Wanderers mistakenly forgot the Stanley Cup at the photographer's house. It was later discovered that the photographer's mother was using it as a flower pot for geraniums!

the end!

Conclusion

I hope you enjoyed the book and had fun telling friends and family your favorite facts! If you liked this book, lend it to someone!

This is the end of our hockey journey for now. But the beautiful thing about sports is that they're infinite games. Every year more hockey games are played, new players break new records, and more funny stories are recorded!

So enjoy this collection, and come back in a few years! You'll realize you've forgotten most of the facts and you'll have the joy of rediscovering them. And by that time, maybe there will be a new volume in this series!